Sunspots

A Narrative Poem

Copyright © 2009 Mary May Burruss

All rights reserved. No part of this book may be reproduced or transmitted in any form or by any means, electronic or mechanical, including photocopying, recording, or by any information storage and retrieval system, without permission from the author.

Sketches by Mary May Burruss

Book Design by Dianne Marcum

Dedication

In memory of my friend Joyce Gobie with whom I played paper dolls and jacks when six years old, and with whom only recently I shared a big belly laugh while reading passages of our purple prose.

Contents

Drumbeat from Outer Space	7
Coming Attractions	19
The First Tears	31
Feeding the Hungry	37
Some of Our Best Friends are Black	43
Contemplation	49
Red Red Rose of Paradise	55
The Dark Shadow of Music	77
Sunstrokes	89
The Magic Music Tree	97
Biscayne Bay	107
The First Goodbye	125
Body Counts	133
In the Spirit of Christmas	139
Young Love That Passes for Love	151
Dark Cloud of God	161
Liberation	177

Drumbeat from Outer Space

Drumbeat from Outer Space

There! Again!
My imagination explodes.
In the distance,
An ominous thrum turns
Blood to ice.
Muscles taut,
I swallow a ton of air
And hold it in.
Heartbeats shudder to a stop.

A pleasure, my professors said.
Mother and Father agreed,
Their contented child, no trouble at all.
They would not recognize me
Decades later a coward
In a darkened bedroom,
Covers pulled to eyebrows.
So this is it, the way one dies.

Again! The urgent summons
Now a soft fluttering pulse
Of fingernails on sheepskin,
Brm-brm-brm
Then stuttering slats of Venetian blinds
Trill in a summer breeze.

Until recently the sound was almost
Indistinguishable
From the normal hum of traffic,
The whine of airplanes overhead
And a chorus of neighborhood
Lawn mowers.

As night approaches
The compelling brm-brm-brm grows shrill,
A penetrating chord that only I can hear.
Eyebrows pinched tight,
Head buried in a down pillow,
My timorous cries muffled.

Please. What is it you want?

David, I call.

My brother David lives a thousand miles north or south.

He believes that love transcends human frailty,

But flourishes best at a distance.

The echo will eat me alive,

Spit me out as a worthless vagrant.

Rancid, decadent, lower than low

Mother had said years ago

Of beggars.

Now, out of earshot,

I beg for mercy.

Soon a column of young men advances,
All of them David,
Faces immobile,
Arms restless, insistent,
Brm-brm-brm.

Suddenly a deafening bottomless
Boom!
If I open the door
The boom will become
A single rupture of earth
That sucks oxygen from my lungs.

And then what?
No more boom,
No purr of daily life,
No gurgle of whiskey,
No trace of a pulse,
No nothing.

Again I cry for David.
If not David who else?
Who has the courage?
Who really gives a damn?

Eventually the pillow
Unfurls from my ears,
Nothing audible now
But the murmur of household machinery,
And the tumble of ice in a crystal goblet.

Again, like yesterday
And the day before,
My neck and scalp are wet.
Eyes hot, burned raw.
By half-past midnight
The steady rhythmic beat
Slowly disappears.

At last I catch my breath and sigh.
Thank you, God.
Of course the thrum will soon return,
Too soon, but not today.
More is expected of me today.
David is unnecessary today,
Thank you, God.
Grayson, the attorney, unnecessary
The Reverend Ford unnecessary
Doctor Kurtz unnecessary
And anyone else with half a brain
All of them unnecessary
Thank you, God, thank you.

Soon I place a black silk strap
On my upper arm
My blood pressure high again.
Up Up Up, beyond outer space.
The figures never go down.
Dr. Kurtz warns me not to play doctor
With inferior products.

You'll live to be a hundred, Dr. Kurtz says.
Kurtz is king of the jungle, proud of his thick mane.
He yawns and glances at his watch,
Patients scheduled in fifteen-minute increments,
Then at my body, a mass of abuses,
Some reparable, some not.
One gets what one pays for.
Today I am paying for my life,
Paying debts in fifteen-minute increments.

My lips practice a wicked smirk.
If Kurtz had bothered to ask
I could have saved us both a lot of stress,
Saved us both an hour or two
Of elevated pressure.
You see, Kurtz old boy, it's this way.
The whole damn universe is falling apart
And I'm leading the charge.

My fist is raised high,
Knuckles grazing the wall.
Charge!

Charge!
Children with toy drums march in place
Brm-brm-brm.
The men bearing arms are not soldiers
But members of my family,
A question in their eyes.
What is it you want, Isabel,
Just tell us what you want.
You order us forward,
But where?

Children make the rules now,
Their superior knowledge
Riding the shoulders of history.
Mozart could not reproduce
The music of their laughter
Nor Shakespeare their artistry,
The years of my childhood
Remembered with ease
But the years in between
Dark mysteries.

Coming Attractions

Coming Attractions

Martha, the first-born sister
Who didn't live beyond pneumonia
At eighteen months,
But remained entombed
In a heavy mahogany oval frame
Over Mother's swayback bed.
No matter where our family lived
Sweet innocent Martha
Witnessed midnight copulation,
Father on top, sweating, struggling
With yards of chiffon between
Mother's yielding thighs.

Three further efforts paid dividends.
First I, Isabel.
Then David
And finally Gilbert.

Gilbert? An afterthought,
God's surprise gift
To parents grown weary of surprises.
Baby brother years too young to join
Conversation at the dinner table.
A brother eager to be loved,
But afraid of David,
Afraid of the moon,
Afraid of loud noises,
Afraid of being wrong,
Yet brave enough to survive
A week in the Everglades
On nothing but rattlesnakes.
Strong enough to land
A four hundred pound shark.

Gilbert perfected the art
Of shedding tears
The blue of his eyes
Pale behind a watery film.

Who struck him, Mother asked.
Indignation burned a hole in the space between us.
Which of you hurt his feelings?
Come to me, baby, come to Mother.

Gilbert did as Mother said,
And joined the church.
If Mother had her way,
She would have given birth to a preacher.
Every family should have a preacher,
A doctor, or a lawyer.
When all else fails, marry character.
When all else failed, I married character.

As a teenager Gilbert abandoned
His interest in the clergy
For a more acceptable
Interest in music and women.

I should have told him
Women aren't worth the loss of sleep.
He would live to regret such a preoccupation.
Better he camp out
In the Everglades
A few days of contemplation.
After all, a man of his sensibilities
Was destined to a life
Devoted to prayer.
Gilbert seldom read anything but the Bible
For pleasure, librettos
A repertoire of Italian lyrics.

We thought he was pious
But in truth, he was drawn to the church
By its music,
Gilbert singing the lead
In the children's choir.
The lead in his high school glee club.
The lead in grand opera.

If only I had let him win at checkers.

Mother still bruised blue
I, Isabel, emerged
Twice as clever as Martha
Twice as beautiful
Twice as virtuous,
To make up for what Martha might have been.
But I wasn't really.
Martha wasn't.
My existence a poor substitute for the real thing
Second best, no matter how gentle,
How generous a spirit,
How agile a mentality.

Friends took one look at my crib.
What? Another girl?
Another disappointment, they said.
Try harder next time.

Mother and Father tried harder next time
Until, months later, halleluiah,
Received what they desired all along,
David
The son who would elevate our family
From obscurity to prominence,
Who would bring distinction,
Respectability,
Pride, honor, dignity.
Now that they conceived a prince
Mother could relax.

No. No. By then
Father had developed
A lusty appetite for copulation,
The springs of their bed
Rhythmically singing
Through closed doors
For the next twenty years.

Love one another, Mother said,
And so we did.
If we argued, one child vanquished,
The other victorious,
She ordered us
Kiss and make up,
A big fat unsanitary
Mushy kiss on the mouth.
Better we behave
Than kiss and make up.
Yuk.

Mother's intuition was more accurate
Than a polygraph.

She bragged about us
And pretended to love us each the same
Though we knew better,
Briefly, after David left home,
She was transformed
No longer our Mother.
Dressed in silk hose and white gloves
Queen of the Missionary Society,
Our indentured parent,
But wore a nightgown until noon,
Made her presence fully dressed for dinner,
Took a walk with Dad among ficus trees,
Or, on special occasions,
Let her fingers glide along piano keys
Exactly as the music was written.

The First Tears

The First Tears

My diary is cluttered with unrelated gibberish.

Gilbert, before he could walk,

Climbed the ladder to the roof.

A nail in David's foot

Itch

Lice

Baptism

Tides

Multiplication tables

Beer

Worms

Spiders

Honor roll

Latin conjugation

And then…

Then?

Don't peek, thank you.

After the first nine chapters

My diary is stained with tears, its pages blank,

Leaving no history of *IT*.

Two *ITS*.

Three.

Three IT-marks carved in cypress

Deep in the Everglades where they remain

Even now, undiscovered,

Thin mottled bark grown like yeast

Over its wounds.

Brm. Brm. Brm.

Thunderstorms,

The urine of wild animals,

Brutal heat

Termites

Ancient scars clawed at

Until written accounts are concealed

Safely within the family.

So! Not as smart as Martha, huh?
Not as remarkable, huh?
But intelligent enough to swear
Vows of secrecy,
Our reputation secure.

No one even guessed
Except God, of course.
God knew everything.
God knew every wicked thought
And more, our good intentions.

Love Thy neighbor, He said
Those responsible were neighbors
On a scale of one to ten,
Insignificant when
Compared to our un-thoroughbred dog
Flax.

Feeding the Hungry

Feeding the Hungry

Flax was tumbleweed
Matted fur powdered in coal dust
Short quick legs
Stomach sweeping the sidewalk
Tail tick-tock east to west
A quick look backwards to check
If he was still chased by wardens.
Like hobos who begged for food
He waddled directly from the railroad
To a big chalky X marked
On porch steps.
Free food here.
Free lodging out back.
Happy children to kiss you on the mouth
And make up for life's injustice.

Flax lapped four pails of faucet water,
Devoured leftovers from Sunday's roast,
Before he stretched in the sun and slept it off.
Mother combed his tangled fur.
Jasmin bathed him in a galvanized laundry tub.
By evening and by secret ballot
Flax wiggled his way into the family circle.

As long as you are responsible, Mother said.
Meaning what, we asked.
Meaning keep him free of ticks and fleas,
Train him not to chase cars,
Clean and fill his water bowl,
Those are your tasks.
David nodded.
I nodded.
We promised.
Jasmin would do these unpleasant things for us
Just as she did everything else but breathe.

Sketched in the sidewalk,
Hopscotch, kick the can
Red Rover, Red Rover
Simon says May I,
Jump rope
Our laughter a happy tune
From dawn to dusk we played,
Flax, yipping and nipping at our heels
Joyful,
Parents joyful.
We children joyful.
Outer space joyful.
None of us would grow old
Like the man next door
Who ordered us off his property.

Well, most of us didn't.

Some of Our Best Friends are Black

Some of Our Best Friends are Black

Jasmin was Birmingham black,
Anonymous.
Our third parent,
Teacher, cook, and advocate.
The smell of her still clings to percale sheets
Twenty years later.

Jasmin boiled greens with ham,
Eggplant to die for
Chopped onion in mashed potatoes
Fried okra.
She ironed linens, a luxury,
Starched cotton underwear,
Even after we told her not to.
Scrubbed the bathtub,
Then, without warning, boarded a bus
Dark and foggy,
Home we supposed

Home with no address.
How could she, Gilbert asked
When she belongs to our family,
We love her right here,
As if there were no *right there*,
With a family of her own waiting.

Jasmin knew when to keep her mouth shut
When to tell Sir, our father.
She helped with our homework
Until the third grade,
When shown an enameled globe of the world.
Good Lord, girl,
All those open spaces
While me and you
We're only germs
The size of roach doo-doo.
I ain't yet been as far as Memphis
Much less those unpronounceable
Faraway places.

While she occupied a throne
In our kitchen and playground
Jasmin was not allowed pain
Nor time off to visit relatives,
Store-bought clothes
Or permission to explore
The globe of her world.

If only she returned for an hour
For one more hug against her limp apron
I would tell her I am sorry.

Contemplation

Contemplation

Old age is the price we pay for
A seat on the aisle.
Better wear a blindfold
Than review the past
As if watching a parade of plaintiffs,
The music of their drums and bugles
Suddenly off key.
Stony eyes fix on mine as they pass.
One by one stare me down,
Until I crumble at the curb,
The parade no longer Sousa's stirring music,
But a procession of failures.

So I'm none of the things expected of me.
When visions of yesterday meander
In and out among daydreams.
A broad smile
should appear on my lips.
Instead I draw a blanket to my neck,
The echo of drumbeats
Unrelenting in my ears.

Brm, brm, brm.
Quiet please,
Or is that too much to ask.

Red Red Rose of Paradise

Red Red Rose of Paradise

Our childhood in Miami was hot and humid.
Beat you, David said.
We raced from the kitchen to back of our lot
And our very own rubber tree,
Its branches so high we could see
Biscayne Bay from our watchtower.

We laughed, paddled and played dead
As we floated to Cuba and back
One day me, one day David swimming ahead
Until Jasmin, waiting on shore, said
Get outta that water before you sprout
Gills and fins.

Tail and ears at attention
Flax romped under our blue umbrella,
Lathered our faces,
Licked salty toes,
Still unsatisfied, tripped us,
His legs twisted among kids' legs.
Then we lay spread eagle,
Itchy blades of Saint Augustine grass
Pricking our bare skin.
We blinked at the blinding sun
Clouds rich as whipped cream
In Jasmin's bowl of meringue.

Our mornings were garish white, silver and gold
Arms and legs sizzling brown
We named the clouds
And remained flat on the ground
While plotting a war from tree to tree
Splintered old crates our fortress,
David declared victory
Over let's-pretend enemy soldiers.

Sometimes Carlos

From two houses down

Came to play

Sometimes Ann Marie, our la-de-da cousin,

When she was allowed,

To play a tamer game of jacks

Or hop scotch.

A soft limestone pebble

Marked the lines in our driveway,

Flax off to the side,

Minding his own business

In a shady hollow under the seesaw.

Jasmin made cream cheese and olive sandwiches

Served on paper plates

For our make believe outdoor feast

When, suddenly,

Ann Marie said she had to go home

Where she ate from honest-to-God imported china.

She threw the limestone pebble and hit Flax,

Who, wakened from blissful dreams,

Yipped, growled at her

And burrowed the ground at her feet.

To avoid him,

Ann Marie spun round and round.

Her arms flailed.

Make him stop!

We giggled ha-ha-ha,

Our laughter boundless.

Flax by then tore into her sandwich.
Ann Marie brushed grass and dirt
From her braided hair
And off her pretty pink skirt.
She smeared lines of hop-scotch and stomped.
Goo-ood bye!
Then in a fit of distemper
She kicked Flax in the rear
Outta my way! I'm outta here!
Flax bounced after her,
Paws flapping in air
Sharp claws carved
A bright pink river
Down Ann Marie's fair cheek.

Backs arched under a blistering sky
We applauded.
Toodledoo, Ann Marie
Go home to your mama
See if we care.
Livid crimson and teary-eyed
Ann Marie squealed.
You just wait, smarty-pants
I'm going to tell my father, so there.

Flax wandered off to a cool spot
Under the rubber tree.
Soon we forgot about Ann Marie
And the thread of blood on her ivory skin.
Thirsty, we went to fasten
A chain to Flax's collar
Before going inside
For a glass of cold lemonade.

Jasmin balanced Gilbert on one hip,
While she boiled starch.
You already give up for the day?
She asked as she filled our glasses.
You children parched?
We drooped over the kitchen table.
Yes, it's hot as hell, David said.

Jasmin jerked David by the arm.
Hush your mouth young man
You know Sir would whup you good
If he knew you talked ugly
Or do something wrong.
She wiped our sweaty faces
On one of Gilbert's clean diapers
Then gave us a hug.
Jasmin couldn't stay mad for long.

We were still indoors, still in the kitchen,
Lazy air filtered through the back screen door,
When a shadow stirred across our driveway
And darkened the linoleum floor.

Jasmin frowned and squinted,
One hand a brim at her brow.
Who dat? Who dat coming this way?
Dat's Ned, David mocked.
Nobody knows how
But he's blood-kin Uncle Ned
Drunk as a skunk again.
I'd seen Ned drunk before
But never up close
Never hauling a heavy sledge-hammer
Like the one now tight in his powerful fist.

We could tell Ned was drunk
By the way he swayed
Discombobulated,
His center of gravity off-course,
His grip on the sledge-hammer
As an extension of his arm,
Its muscle twice normal size.
He recovered from swaying
Only to stagger off the left edge of the drive
And barely caught himself before he wobbled
Or swayed to the right.

Brrm.

Jasmin, smelling trouble, gathered us into her apron

Its printed flowers faded in dishwater and lye.

Don't you kids move.

Don't you dare make a sound or ask why.

When Uncle Ned got close, just outside the screen door,

We could see the determination

In his blazing beet-red eyes

And heard swear words,

Nastier than any David knew.

Spit bubbled like soapsuds in Ned's mouth

As his gravelly voice bellowed.

Where da hell…Fluckin dog…where you at?

We grasped Jasmin's apron tighter,
Her wrinkled thin hands pinned us
To her wrinkled thin dress.
Lips trembling, she hummed a hymn
And nudged us to the sink
Where she could see out the window
What Uncle Ned was up to,
Though we had already guessed.

Straining at his neck,
Flax tore from one tree to the next.
Ever so often the chain caught on the wire
That held him in check
As he yipped with confusion and pawed.
His nervous eyes begged for help.
Then, when Uncle Ned came near
Flax drew his ears tight, tail tucked low,
Until he was no more
Than a quivering ball of fear.

Stop Uncle Ned, we said,
Make him leave!
Jasmin urged us into the closet
With brooms and mops,
As if playing a game.
But we'd hidden there before
And escaped to watch
From the back screen door.

Get away from here, we yelled. *Go home!*
At once Jasmin's face came within inches of ours.
She pinched my chin.
You itching to see the business end
Of that hammer up close?
If you know what's good for you
You'll shut your sassy mouth.

Ned's sturdy wrist choked up on the hammer,

Lifted it high, swung it low,

And cracked the bones in Flax's head.

Godagoddum dog!

Again and again the hammer made an arc

And came down hard.

No-count animule!

A wound in Flax's stomach bled.

Let- that-be-a-lesson!

Blood gushed from Flax's tongue,

His neck shiny dark.

In a swift and steamy motion

Jasmin released her hand from my mouth

Then flung the back screen door wide.

Finally, no longer able to remain silent, she screamed.

Go away, mistah, go back where you come from!

Suddenly Ned paused,

The hammer overhead paused.

Birds, clouds, tides and God's love all paused.

Zat you nigger?

Hurt my baby Ann Marie would ya?

For good measure

He swung the hammer once more,

Then let it drop against the chain.

Guess again.

Still unsteady, he tripped over his own feet

And left.

Jasmin quaked head to toe.
Gilbert sobbed,
His little hands still locked at Jasmin's neck
David bit his lip 'til it was raw.
I whimpered and slid to the floor.
As soon as Uncle Ned disappeared
Across the street,
Jasmin rushed to the rubber tree
And sat on the blood-spattered grass,
Flax's lifeless body in her lap.
As she rocked back and forth
Giant tears rolled from Jasmin's eyes.
Lordy, dear God in Heaven.
Lordy, Lordy, Lordy she said.

She wrapped Flax in her apron,
Its sash soon crusty stiff and red.
Jasmin breathed deep,
Shook her head side to side
And ordered us indoors to get towels.
Frozen in place, I hesitated
My pulse clickety-click,
My throat dry, voiceless.
Git! Do what you're told, Jasmin said.
This ain't no occasion to wring your hands.

We brought the towels.

David helped Jasmin dig a deep hole

Out back near our packing crates and fortress.

You want to say a prayer, it's all right, Jasmin said.

Though our words came in sputters

We said a prayer.

When we came to *forever and ever amen*

Jasmin responded *Amen*.

Amen, God help him, Amen

Amen God forgive him, Amen

For he knowed not what he done Amen.

Oh yes he did, I said. *He knew damn well.*

Jasmin glared at me,

Another swollen tear fell to her feet.

You want to shovel some dirt in over him, Isabel

You go right ahead.

That's what grown folks do.

That's how it's done.

<u>It</u> was saying goodbye to Flax.
<u>It</u> was a happy day suddenly heartbreaking.
<u>It</u> was beautiful turned ugly.
Music turned sour,
Sunshine turned midnight black,
Love turned to bile.

Jasmin picked Gilbert off the ground
His starched romper bloody and wet.
His cries were like hiccups, a mournful sound.
Jasmin stroked him 'til he sighed asleep.
Don't none of you grieve, she said.
Don't trade a pure heart for evil.
Don't think about it ever no more.
She hugged us so close it hurt.
Then she left us alone in the kitchen
While she scrubbed red-splattered concrete out back.

Some things even Jasmin couldn't make possible.
I thought of *it*,
Not just that day
But almost every day of my life.

The Dark Shadow of Music

The Dark Shadow of Music

Our father,
The person Jasmin called Sir
Mother called sweetheart
And we called Dad
Was deaf, ever since the war.
His buddies, including Uncle Ned,
Pulled him from a burning plane
Before enemy troops arrived.

He loved aviation.
Now he couldn't fly.
Instead he was promoted

From field hospital to stateside
And finally home
Where he never stopped feeling
The sputter of his bullet-riddled plane,
Never stopped thanking his buddies,
Never stopped hearing the whistle of bombs
Over slumbering space,
Never stopped loving our mother.
The war is over, he said, over.

He might better have celebrated, but suddenly
Dad would not hear Gilbert count to ten,
Would not hear Jasmin call us to dinner,
Would not hear the chirp of birds outside his window.

By magic his ears remained sensitive
To the strings of David's guitar,
And the ivory keys of our baby grand piano.
From dawn to dusk our house
Hummed with music.

Dad hoped David would play football and lift weights
However, to develop the right side of his brain,
It wouldn't hurt to know music as well
And so David and I studied with Miami's best,
Miss Florence Getz
Who taught only six blocks up the street.
She welcomed new students
Because Mr. Getz suffered from diabetes,
They were members of genteel poverty.

We took turns,

One of us at the keyboard with Miss Florence,

The other waiting with Mr. Getz in his greenhouse.

When we weren't playing music

We learned about exotic plants,

Proper soil and cross-pollination.

David learned everything Mr. Getz already knew

About cuttings, grafts and succulents.

After arriving back home

He planted a sickly garden of his own

Started from seeds Mr. Getz gave him.

On one particular day of our lesson
David struggled through etudes and scales
While I waited in the cool greenhouse
Where Mr. Getz re-potted bromeliads.
I yawned and shifted my feet.
Not interested today? Mr. Getz asked.
Come here my sweet
I'll show you something you'll never forget.
The Red Rose of Paradise.
First he unfastened his belt,
Then opened the zippered placket to reveal
His swollen flesh.
I gulped.
Touch it, he said. *Kiss it.*
He stroked my leg.
Kiss the Red Rose of Paradise.
Don't be afraid.
My eyes grew big as ostrich eggs.

Brm-brm.

Next, closer yet,

His girth pinned me to the workbench.

One massive hand snagged the elastic of my underwear.

The other moved inch by inch down my body.

He caressed my stomach and lower,

To places never touched before.

Don't, I said.

Lips moist, he smiled.

Paradise, dear. Paradise, The Red Rose of Paradise.

Kiss-kiss.

His wet mouth came down hard on my lips.

His fingers crawled across my pelvis

Finally I twisted to escape Mr. Getz

And his exotic flowers.

Outside the greenhouse

Miss Florence was calling.

Your turn Isabel

I smoothed my clothes.

In passing David,
I squinted a solemn cautionary message.
For the next hour the metronome tick tick ticked.
Miss Florence scowled,
Your chords are discordant, my dear, tee hee.
Did you forget to practice this week?
Your work is not up to standard.

Though I felt sick,
I managed to walk home
Where Dad greeted us at the door,
His soft gray eyes filled with happiness.
Ah, music. What would we do without music?

To please my dad
I continued to take piano lessons.
Dave swore on the Bible he wouldn't blab.
If our father knew, he would kill Mr. Getz.
From that day forward
While I rehearsed a barcarole,
David remained in the music room
Near the empty canary cage and goldfish bowl
And I remained indoors for him.

Mr. Getz taught me more
Than the Red Rose of Paradise.
Though music lessons with Miami's best
Were unbearable then.
Mozart's music wasn't to blame,
But Mr. Getz.
We'd been raised on Mother's lullabies,
All things musical.
Our parents taught us, not Florence Getz,
That music was beautiful, sublimely beautiful.

While Mr. Getz got off light that day,
I never forgot his gnarled fingers,
The sting of his beard on my tender skin,
The curdled smell of his breath,
Never forgot the stabbing fear
Of ever being alone with him again.

His time would come.

Sunstrokes

Sunstrokes

Were we happy? Why not?
Our winters mild, summers hot.
Nothing special. So what?
We didn't know how hot it could get
Our scalp and brows shiny with sweat.
Arms brown, eyes squinting into a white hot sun
Our clothes wrinkled and wet.
Happy? You call that happy?

After June we played tennis
Unless it rained.
Our hand-me-down bicycles knew the way
From Matheson Hammock to Key Biscayne.
We pedaled through garish halls
Of Poinciana trees.

Pods of seeds cracked below

Long-stemmed ferns clung to limestone walls

Hot tar pavement mottled orange or red

The sky to the east a rich indigo.

West, over the Everglades

A thunderhead.

We prayed for cool water, a gentle breeze.

Happy? Well, somewhat happy.

With our dad we fished inland

And trolled among mangroves

Murky and thick with mosquitoes,

Alligators, blue-clawed crabs, oyster beds

If we were lucky, and the tide was right

Up and down Keys, to the Gulf Stream or Fowey Light

Here and there dazzling flamingos

Swooped overhead.

We cast for snook in Florida Bay

And actually caught fish

That Jasmin fried the following day.

We undressed in the kitchen,

Smelly wet clothes piled high on the floor.

And hoped no one peaked

Through the back screen door.

David cleaned the boat 'til late

While I sorted tackle or unused bait.

Our deaf father still smiled

As he had since morning

Never missing a spoken word,

What he guessed, but hadn't heard.

Were we ridiculously, fantastically happy?

Of course, we were.

Until…

Predictably *until*
Life feeds on *until*
Until the Second Coming
Until we graduate
Until we can afford it
Until Daddy comes home
Until next winter.

We are unprepared

For the onslaught of unknowns

For too much rain

Too many cars on the road

Too much booze at the party.

David, Gilbert and I were happy *until*...

Until Uncle Ned turned childhood upside down

Jasmin took to the streets

Young men went to war in Viet Nam

Our lives happy *until* then.

The Magic Music Tree

The Magic Music Tree

Palm trees thrive in the Tropics.
Skinny trunks forty feet high
Their fruit inaccessible
Lacy green fronds reach for the sky.

Our mulberry tree was as tall
But not as slim
We climbed lofty branches
To gather purple berries
That stained our clothes
And took foolish chances
As we swung limb to limb.

Our pine tree, however, was common and plain,
Pliable wire led from the garage
Wound around its brittle bark, then knotted.
Jasmin pinned wet laundry to the wire
Until Dad bought an electric drier
And we brought a length of chain
As a run where Flax could exercise
Or escape vicious sun and rain.

Bored and hot, having spent the day
Riding my bike to Biscayne Bay,
I paused at the tree to catch my breath.
Flax blinked, then settled back to a torpid snooze.
Suddenly I was surrounded by music,
Mysterious sounds Flax seemed not to hear.
The Tree! Our ugly pine tree made music!
My ear pressed tight against scratchy bark
Yes, indeed. On my cheek pitted marks
From the tree, music crystal clear.

At first I didn't recognize its tune,
Chopin, I thought, Moonlight Sonata.
Yet this was early afternoon!
Not evening, Chopin in the heat of day.
Music had never before been so moving or magic.
The tree possessed divine powers.
I raced indoors to tell David
Though I didn't find him until dinner.
Guess what!
Music! From the pine tree.
You'd never guess. Chopin and Bach.
Yeah? Prove it, he said.

Soon after, the tree played yet another tune
Parts of Carmen, by Bizet
David tried to hide his excitement.
It's a secret, I said, between you and me.
He promptly told Dad, who pushed back his chair
And smiled playfully.
A phenomena, he said.
Every once in awhile a wire transmits
Radio signals through the air
Atmospheric conditions especially rare.

I was unconvinced.
Dad was trying to make David feel big
At my expense.
Then, as Dad noticed my downcast eyes,
He came to grips with my surprise.
Though ugly and useless, he said
Our pine tree is phenomenally magic
The only one of its kind.
You won't find another like it
South of the Mason Dixon Line

An illogical explanation.
The magic tree would bring happiness
From generation to generation
To those who appreciate fine music.
Dad continued.
Isabel, you discovered a universal truth.
Only those who hear the pine tree's magic music
Will be admitted to heaven.

Religious since birth, Mother stared at him.
Mother believed God floated to earth
On a billowy cloud.
He would select only saintly souls for salvation
Then cradle in his arms those few allowed
And vanish into the sky again.
Mother's God had nothing to do with music
Broadcast from a local radio station.

When no one was looking
I visited the pine tree,
My ear touching its bark,
And sometimes slipped out after dark
To be with God and music.

I kept those nighttime visits a secret
Between me and God.
And told no one, for fear that
He would take my place in heaven.
Told no one at all until Gilbert was sick,
And needed all the help he could get.

While everyone else slept

I entered Gilbert's musty room

Touched my lips and signaled

Quiet!

Gilbert's glazed eyes slowly opened.

He kicked a cotton quilt,

Then looped a limp feverish arm across my shoulder.

Pajama bottoms sagged on his bony hips.

We stumbled through the house

To the back screen door

And finally reached the tree.

Gilbert hugged himself as if cold,

So I showed him how to listen.

And he did as he was told.

Music? he asked.

Yes! Don't worry about saving your soul any more.

You'll be safe with God in heaven now.

Every life could use a touch of magic.

Biscayne Bay

Biscayne Bay

Father bought boats
The way some people bought shoes,
When in the mood,
Usually a boat he could use alone.
Everyone should learn to rely on himself, he said.
Good for one's soul.
An hour alone at sea
Cleared one's head of life's debris.

David liked the open runabout best
With a big Evinrude outboard motor
That at the first opportunity
He tested.
David liked speed of any kind.
Cars, airplanes, boats.

Gilbert, much younger, turned white with fear.
And hunkered low, breathing bilge
Rather than let his older brother
See him shiver and shake.
Gilbert had an abiding respect for dry land.

One March afternoon
Dad let Dave take charge of the boat.
We were in high school then,
Old enough for adult responsibilities.

Dad had not seen Uncle Ned for years
Until they met at a grocery store.
He's changed, Dad said to us later.
And furthermore, he attends AA now.
Noting our silence, he added.
Hate is a deadly disease.
A gentleman forgives.
He turns the other cheek.
More silence.
Dad smiled. *So you choose to hate.*
He shrugged.

I choose to invite Ned to our picnic next week.

My jaw dropped.

David gasped.

Mother's voice cracked. *You what?*

Dad coughed. *He seemed interested in our new boat,*

So I suggested Saturday.

At our house, David owned Saturday
Dad trusted him on the water alone now.
Won't there be too many? Mother said,
A touch of hope in her voice.
Dad shook his head.
We'll make it to the island and back in two trips.
Dave can handle the motor.
Dave's chest grew three sizes in two minutes.

For days Mother had planned our food
But now she wouldn't join us, she said.
At the last minute her head ached.
We knew better than insist.
Mother's constitution was fragile at best.
Her headaches existed
At her convenience.

Gilbert wishy-washed.
He would rather remain at home, in bed.
But didn't dare give David
Reason to tease him later.
Ned will meet us at the pier, Dad said.

Saturday's weather cooperated
A piercing white sky,
The bay glazed, sprinkled with sun-diamonds.
Traffic along the causeway zipped by.
Everyone cheerful, even Uncle Ned
Who met us as promised
Promptly at the pier.
He wore a printed green shirt
Over a bright red bathing suit.
With a big childish grin,
He loaded baskets of sandwiches and fruit.

Hello, he said
As if we'd seen each other the day before.
David smiled back,
Then winked at me,
A wink nobody else was meant to see,
The sort of wink I couldn't ignore.

How about Dad and Gilbert go first,
To start the fire, Dave said.
I'll run them over to set up a tent.
You wait here, Isabel, with Uncle Ned.

Daddy's face was radiant.
All was right with the world.
He had forgiven Uncle Ned
For killing Flax,
His children, though no longer babies,
Still spent a day outdoors with him.
Life was beautiful,
More than a man deserved.

Dad eased down onto the middle plank,
Facing Dave, at the stern.
Gilbert unhooked the line
And pushed off from the pier,
Then lay stomach down on the bow,
One arm trailing over the side.

Meanwhile I waited with Uncle Ned
As the boat disappeared
Under the bridge and beyond.
Ripples of wake rocked a skiff nearby.

Uncle Ned searched billowing white clouds.
Pretty day, he said.

My answer was a mouth full of mush. *Yes.*

Our legs dangled from the pier.
I stared straight ahead.
Any minute Uncle Ned would produce a sledgehammer.
He would strike me, here, here and here.
Arms, legs, my brittle bones.

So what that he never got drunk any more!
So what he had repented!
So what we were taught to forgive!
I was sixteen
And wanted to live forever.
David wanted to coach football.
Gilbert wanted to sing.
To tell the truth
Uncle Ned had no right
To expect anything but silence.

Nice skiff you got there, he said.

Yes. How's Ann Marie?

Fine, just fine.

I didn't want Ann Marie fine, just fine.
I wanted Ann Marie homely and fat
Clumsy, untalented,
A despicable brat.

Soon between concrete pillars
The boat reappeared.
The noise of its motor
Loud and sure.
David waved,
Then secured the boat.

Quickly we loaded the rest of our gear.
Uncle Ned rocked the boat
As he settled on the middle seat.
I shoved us off from the pier
And sat forward,
Eyes trained on the horizon.

First Dave circled east in the bay,
Then gaining speed, veered north
Toward the bridge
With its concrete pilings.
We knew from experience
When the tide was high
To duck before passing
Between its barnacled pillars.

Meanwhile Uncle Ned's green shirt
Fluttered in the wind.
David moved left to right to see around him.
How about taking off your shirt, David yelled.
The boat sliced through smooth blue water,
Its spray chilling my bare, warm skin.
David turned the throttle higher.
What's that? Uncle Ned asked.
Your shirt. I can't see up ahead for your shirt.

Still facing Dave, Uncle Ned suddenly stood in the boat

His feet unsteady.

Sure. Sorry, he said.

He removed his shirt first one arm,

Then another, then over his head.

We were almost to the bridge

And the pilings,

David and I ready to duck

When Uncle Ned wobbled,

Struggled with his shirt

And shuffled sluggish feet.

The shirt was almost completely off his body

As we came to the bridge.

Instinctively David and I ducked low.

The bow safely entered a narrow channel

Then a bone-crushing wham!

Spun the boat sideways.

The impact of Ned's body
As it struck the bridge
Jarred the boat and motor.
Uncle Ned was thrown against the keel
And knocked Dave backward.
Quickly, regaining control,
Dave tightened his grip on the tiller.
I screamed. *David*!
But I knew,
And David knew that I knew.
Brrm-brrm.

We sped back over the bay

Glided to the ramp

Where I screamed while facing the noonday sun.

Somebody help us!

Somebody call 911!

David cut the motor,

Around us a momentary stillness

Before fishermen rushed to help.

They placed a blanket over Uncle Ned.

Anyone call emergency? Dave asked.

Another fisherman folded Uncle Ned's green shirt.

And wedged it under his head,

A stranger's voice hardly audible.

I did, but it's no use.

Terrible, terrible accident, terrible.

The poor guy's dead.

Later, after hours of official hullabaloo,
I helped Dave wash the boat.
He turned on the hose for a minute or two,
Then lifted one forefinger
And motioned for me to keep it to myself.
That's one, he whispered.

The First Goodbye

The First Goodbye

No one is given his choice
Of family.
We are not allowed a voice in
Where we are born or when.
If given the choice,
We'd choose the one we have again.

David and I drew blinds
Against the sunshine of youth
To watch the future unfold.
We were eager, inventive,
Bold and a little bit anxious.
Then heroes of the New Frontier
Broke the bonds of the stratosphere
And planted a flag on the moon.
By changing the course of history
We too would be heroes soon.

We would conquer the mystery of disease
Build skyscrapers,
Write poetry.
Instead, with our first taste
Of things to come,
We answered the call of a distant drum,
Its mournful beat, a moratorium
On common sense.

One morning women's lib
Civil rights, civil wrongs,
The next day war,
Dangerous drugs, dirty songs.
Half of Cuba migrated to Miami
And drove the Haitians north.
We dodged, and debated,
Drank cheap booze.
Daily disaster on the daily news.

And so we marched, we chanted
To the pulse of that mournful drum
Hell no we won't go!
We shall overcome!
Overcome what we didn't know.
Parents regretted being parents
As fumes of marijuana
Filled our lungs,
The world belonged to the young.
If nothing else,
David, Gilbert and I were young.

From year to year tensions grew.
Ours the excitement,
Ours the fear, ours the pain,
Ours an overnight stay in a prison cell
An up-close view of Viet Nam
Old Geezers in Washington
Didn't give a damn,
We would die for their cause.

As Jasmin cleaned room to room
She followed the news on television.
Crosses burned in Birmingham.
Frothing dogs lunged and lurched.
Frothing policemen, frothing fire hoses,
Little black schoolgirls bombed in church,
Someone killed almost every night.
Paused to watch, Jasmin
Raised scrawny fingers to the light.
Those fingers could do more than scrub,
They could alter the globe of the world.

Even Jasmin could march,
Jasmin could burn buildings and break the law,
Jasmin could drink from a fountain For Whites Only
Even Jasmin had a cause.
She held my face between clammy palms,
Leaned down low and kissed my brow.

Be a good girl, Isabel,
I'll be going now.
I ain't got forever.

My heart skipped a beat.
What about Mother?
Mother can't cook
I'd lose my appetite.
What about Dad?
He wants his shirts pressed right
The way you do the sleeves.
What about Gilbert?
Mother leaves it to you
To tend Gilbert during one of his spells.
What about David?
He thinks he's grown but still needs advice.
I swallowed, my heart suddenly cold as ice.
And what about me, Isabel?

Jasmin's fingers-tips trembled on my cheek.
I'm counting on you, Isabel.

Body Counts

Body Counts

Whoever heard of a happy war?
Nobody knows what he's fighting for
Yet young boys fight, and grown men kill.
Enemy soldiers learn the same skills.
Corpsmen count the dead,
And call for more to fill their ranks,
David, when recruited, said *Thanks but no thanks.*
What? Me kill a man I don't even know?
I wasn't born a clump of cannon fodder.
Hell no, I won't go.
With odds like that I'll blow this dump
And get the hell out.
Canada, Oh Canada. Here I come.
Canada or bust!

Mother, in shock, took to her bed.
Daddy adjusted his hearing aid.
What was that my oldest boy said?
His offspring, his blood, his first-born son!
He grabbed David by the neck and
Nailed him to the bedroom door.
Coward! Disgrace! Shame!
A son of mine no more!
Then, seeing the misery in David's eyes,
Let go of him, and cried.
Lord knows I tried to make a man out of you.
Do whatever it is you have to do.
Remember, be safe, wherever you are.

Gilbert, who'd been nervously watching, gulped.
When David goes can I have his old guitar?

One by one David's classmates fell
In Viet Nam, a foreign mass of muddy turf
Even I had a hard time finding
On David's globe of the earth.

I can't say I was exactly proud of my brother then,
But at least he'd live to come home again.

In the Spirit of Christmas

In the Spirit of Christmas

Home for the holidays
I finished shopping for Christmas gifts,
Purchased, wrapped and tagged,
Perfume for Mother, books for Dad.
A sweater for Jasmin, like the one she had
Years ago and wore into rags.

Carlos, too, would return from college.
Two weeks of wall-to-wall embraces,
Two memorable weeks of music and dancing,
Two weeks of slow farewells.

This was the sweet breath of an infant
Before waking from sound slumber.
The hush of a church
Before the first vibrations of organ and choir.
The eerie silence of a battlefield
Before fire explodes from enemy guns.

This was the last golden hour of desire.
Carlos was leaving school to enlist,
His education on hold.
Uncle Sam needs me, he said.
Uncle Sam needs a few good men.
After dark he told me he loved me.
Before noon, told me again.
His kisses still warm on my lips
When Dad asked me to go with him
To deliver gifts to Jasmin.

Please. Don't go, Mother said.
I'll phone ahead and tell her to use the bus
And come here.
I'll bake an extra ham
For her to take home to share.
Haven't you watched television?
Have you seen the pandemonium?
Riots and marches, someone shot there
When simply reading the meter.
Those people, those good-for-nothing impostors.

They aren't our black folks at all
But from out of town, up north somewhere.
Daddy laughed and gently smothered her with kisses.
No, precious. That would never do.
Trust us. Isabel and I aren't new at this.
We'll be back soon to decorate.

Not exactly what I had in mind that day.
Dad and I packed the car with gifts
And stopped on our way for gas.
The attendant warned us not to go further.
He scratched his head.
Not this chicken, brother.
If I was you I wouldn't be caught dead
Over yonder in Liberty City,
Not today, not with them hot-head, politicking
Demonstrators up to no good.

With a broad smile Daddy wished him Merry Christmas

And drove slowly, having second thoughts.

Crowds of blacks, young and old,

Men, women and children

Overflowed sidewalks

Stumbled on curbs,

Gathered on grassless lawns,

Then slapped the car as we passed.

Tight-lipped, Daddy mumbled. *Lock your door, Isabel.*

Jasmin lived upstairs, above a store.

We couldn't go further for the milling horde.

Yellow police tape blocked the intersection.

Black men tossed grapefruit from third floor balconies.

A lone policeman chewed toothpicks,

Nervously caressed his pistol,

Loud speakers blared hard rock and gospel.

Justice! Now or never. Justice! Freedom!
Barefoot boys burned newspapers in dumpsters.
Soon the fire spread to one of the shacks nearby.
Get whitey!

Three or four older men surrounded our car
And jolted it, harder and harder, side to side.
A fire truck's siren screamed in our ears
As it careened around a corner.
Get whitey!

More fruit pelted the pavement. Garbage too.
From a narrow alley, empty tin cans flew,
Firecrackers pow-powed.
Laughter as loud as a bomb.
Then a single bass drum marked time,
And the clash of cymbals, shiny brass.
Rows of demonstrators at the underpass
Marched forward.

Justice! Now or never! Freedom!

There, leading the charge,
And holding one end of a cloth banner, Jasmin,
Our Jasmin, in white Sunday silk,
A size too large, sagging at the hips and thighs,
Her voice insistent, shrill.
A Jasmin we hardly recognized.

Justice!

Upon seeing us, she dropped the banner
And clapped her knees.
Sir! Isabel! What you doin' here!
Daddy held a gift up to the windshield for her to see.

By then pop bottles shot from a barricade
Shattered glass blocked the path of the short parade.
Meanwhile our car continued to rock.
Gun it, daddy, let's get the hell out.

The smile faded on Daddy's mouth.
Are you sure your door is locked?
He was still holding the sweater wrapped in shiny gold
For Jasmin to see.

Fleshy lips pressed on the surface of the windshield,
A dirty boy stomach down on the hood,
His tongue coated with bits of wet food.
Leave that gentleman alone, Jasmin shouted.
Daddy forced open the car door.
Keep the motor running, he said.
Be ready to floor it.

He leapt from the car,
Jasmin rushing toward him
Her outstretched arms pleading,
As I slid behind the wheel.
Dad stumbled over fire hoses,
Christmas gifts falling to the pavement,
Split open, splintered, contents exposed.

Dad's feet tangled in green and red glitter.
Water balloons splashed up ahead.
Half-filled beer bottles sailed through air,
One of them striking Daddy broadside
With a thump, just above his ear.

Jasmin roared.
Sir! Sir! She glared at the balcony above.
Stoppit you fool! Git down from there!

Black men rocking our car retreated
And helped Jasmin carry Dad to the back seat.
She paused just long enough to stroke my cheek.
I'm sorry, she said. *Git! Hurry!*
Her fingers fluttered high. *Let this car onto the street!*
As I gunned the car, and tried to escape,
The bumper finally burst through yellow tape.
An older boy spit a wad of phlegm
Then lowered his pants to show his contempt.

Halfway home, I slowed to the legal speed,
From time to time checked the rear view mirror
To find my Dad on the leather seat.
Stay awake, Dad. We'll be home soon.
Mother is waiting for you to help with the tree.
Still cold with fear,
At the first opportunity
I reached behind to the seat in the rear,
And drew back a bloody hand.
Hang on Dad. We're almost there.

I didn't know then,
And still don't know,
Why the gentlest in our family
Was the first to go.

Young Love That Passes for Love

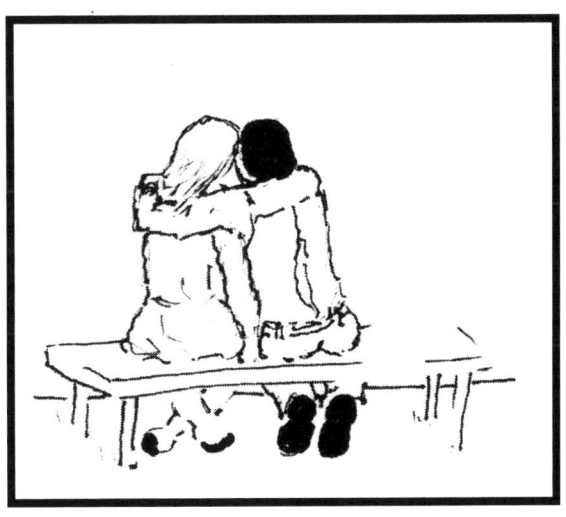

Young Love That Passes for Love

My roommates and I should have been studying.
Our parents sent us to college to study.
But we studied far weightier subjects
Than scholars had in mind.
In small groups and large
We discussed clothes, religion,
Boys, dances, fraternities,
Weekend football games, sex,
Philosophy, and, yes, almost daily,
We talked about love.

I glanced beyond a stained glass window
And noticed a young couple,
Lying in the dark of the dormitory lawn,
Their bare feet illuminated in a dim yellow light.
What did they know, or need to know about love,
When I was an authority.

The heart is a waterwheel that generates love
And pumps sweet syrup through throbbing veins.
Love inhaled through pores
Returns threefold,
In a child's innocent laughter,
A mother's embrace,
A father's daily toil.
A fully-grown body barely contains
The volume of love generated.
The more given, the more appears to take its place,
A surplus on display at the public bazaar.
Love, not for sale, but given freely.
Discounted. Rebated. Guaranteed.
Like the game of secrets, unrecognized,
When passed on, person to person,
One's universe suddenly flooded with love.

Love penetrates the rays of a summer sun,
It spawns the power of oceans tides,
Love hides among shadows of mighty mountains,
And lingers in the simple songs of our music tree,
Every drop of rain is heavy with love.

Love is the sweetness that
Leaves us thirsting for more.
Neither hate nor bitterness
Storms its gates,
But is turned away,
Love's mild climate hostile
To adversity.

Wipe that silly grin off your face, Isabel,
This is serious stuff, all about love.

I tried and half succeeded.

Lips tightly pressed,

Mouth turned up only slightly.

I knew a thing or two about love,

Serious stuff.

No one knew *all* about love.

My love overflowed the immediate family

To include history teachers,

Athletes, doctors,

Friends at summer camp,

A perpetual fountain that spread in cool wet circles

Throughout the neighborhood.

Just beyond a hedge of hibiscus,
Unsuspecting Carlos,
Beautiful carefree Carlos,
Given the full force of pounding wave
After pounding wave
Of love as we danced to music from Havana,
Love as we munched on Cuban pastry,
Love as we counted stars on a starless night,
Balmy midnights, fiery towers of love,
Arms outstretched, eager,
Inner thighs tender, smoldering,
Lips bruised from hours of torrid passion.
An endless, overwhelming love
Packed in canvas duffle bags,
In pockets of hand-woven woolen scarves
In words carefully selected for love-letters,
Air-mailed directly to Viet Nam
Then returned, unopened,
A stranger having stamped perfumed envelopes
<u>Dead</u>. Carlos dead of war wounds
While fighting for his chosen new country.

For hope, for his future and mine.
Next to his heart a bloodied, dog-eared photograph
Carlos and I, face-to-face, smiling,
Serious stuff.

My love flows sluggishly north now,
To David in Canada.
To my mother's bedside
Where she moans, prays, and whispers
Sweet love-words to my dead father.
To Gilbert, on the stage of an opera house abroad,
Wherever his silver voice leads him.
To the memory of what might have been,
Brave Carlos' blood and mine flowing upstream together.

Though my heart never stopped generating love,

My body is too numb to feel it,

Too numb for marriage or motherhood.

My waterwheel is frozen hard, my uterus frozen too.

I am needed now,

Being needed is better than nothing.

Dark Cloud of God

Dark Cloud of God

Mother said she smelled
Ozone in a change of weather,
And I believed her
Just as I believed in my music tree.
No harm could come from such a fantasy.

I was home for good then
After six years away.
Nothing was normal that autumn day.
Gilbert was in New York at Julliard.
Mother found it hard to say goodbye to her baby,
The last of her children to leave her nest.
Just you and me now, Isabel
A tragedy,
As if I weren't as valuable as the rest of the family.

The day before was blustery,
Gentle whiffs of air growing strong
Then a suspenseful calm that hung about,
Waiting to strike off and on.

Sweat glistened on my neck
My blouse stuck to my skin,
Underwear itchy,
Face flushed shiny from brow to chin,
Now and then a furious wind
That didn't last,
The morning sky bright and hot,
By late afternoon overcast.

Dressed in a filmy robe,
Mother listened to weather reports.
Finally she smiled, her happiness unrestrained,
It's coming, Isabel.
The hurricane is coming our way.
She sighed and went to the dining room
To watch tinseled rain

As it pelted the hedges and windowpane.
When awaiting a storm,
Daddy and David had secured the house
And now the job was mine.
Mother might brace the alamanda vine,
She could hold shutters while I fastened them tight.
She might, but she didn't.
She could, but didn't.
Instead like a child, she leaned into the wind
Arms embracing the world
A current of air whipping her gown,
Thin fabric clinging as she turned around.
Just think, Isabel, the sign we hoped for.

No, I said, *You hoped for.*
Again I struggled with shutters.

Mother's eyelashes fluttered.

Yes. I hoped for a sign from God.

He will descend in a cloud, Isabel

Then swoop us into his gentle arms.

She appeared surrounded by light as she spun,

A radiant smile turned upward, to the sunless sky.

Believe me, Isabel. By midnight, we shall be in Heaven.

Please, Mother, you scare me.

Her big hazel eyes shone in the gray dusk.

Her head buried in my neck.

Don't be afraid, dear, we'll be with your father.

Our Heavenly Father?

Yes. Him too.

Hand me those butterfly nuts.
Really, this is a man's job.
My muscles were sore from lifting shutters.

She was still leaning into the wind
Her body a lavender sail floating in space.
Bother the shutters, Isabel.
She sat on the picnic bench, chin on knees,
The gown tucked, but still billowing.
We'll be together. Just imagine.

I imagined, but didn't like the sudden discovery
That Mother was incoherent,
She had lost touch with reality.
I sobbed. Wet hair lashed my face.
When the last shutter was in place
I huddled beside Mother on the picnic bench,
Snuggled close, our shoulders drenched.

Come inside, Mother.
Let me fix dinner while we still have power.
Change into dry clothes.
By then roiling black clouds swept overhead.
Lightning zig-zagged green and blue.
Rain cascaded down garden walls.
Come along, Mother, before I'm as wet as you.

Soon the power went out. We could hardly see.
No air conditioning, no stove, no television,
No cold milk, no hot coffee or tea.
I placed a portable radio near the kitchen sink.
Outside, one of the shutters came loose
And banged against the quaking house.
Trees, growing up a stucco wall
Groaned and creaked.
With every flash of blue lightning
I could make out the music tree,
A pine, bent double, stripped of needles.

The mulberry tree, too old to fight back, splintered,

Fell sideways, its root system on edge

Power lines tangled, flying free.

A washtub skimmed across water

And stopped at the hedge.

In the distance, streetlights flickered.

I made a temporary bed of quilts on the floor.

Mother said thanks, but she'd take a flashlight

And go to bed.

By then every timber whistled.

With a roar, something hit the porch.

I watched the destruction from the shutterless window

Until a small metal street sign came our way.

Jagged shards of glass shone in the lightning glow.

Water slowly seeped over the threshold.

Something banged, over and over,

With each stiff blast of deafening wind.

I fixed the radio close to my ear.

As if the sound of a human voice

Made the ordeal tolerable

I was not alone, after all

The only surviving specimen on our planet.

Clashing and clanging was steady now, hypnotic.

I must have dozed, because soon

The wind weakened, banging and creaking diminished.

Outside, a gray hazy sky.

The worst of the hurricane had passed

And I was still alive, though wet, from the soaked quilt.

Legs doubled under me, I called.

Mother?

I went from one half-dark room to another.

The water in our toilets sloshed, and made sucking noises.

Mother?

And finally to her bedroom.

Her bed was still made, a little pink pillow

In its usual place.

Mother?

Frantic now, I opened closets,

Peaked behind shower curtains,

Under beds, behind couches, every imaginable space.

Then wrapped an old plastic tablecloth over my head.

I forced open a French door.

Mother!

I called louder this time.
Sudden gusts of wind almost knocked me down.
Leaves continued to fall, bushes flat
Boards, papers, tarpaulins, littered the lawn,
Transformers spit blue.
Mother!

I found her in Dad's tool shed.
Her skin ghostly, eyes haunted.
Mother, come inside.
What are you doing out here?

She looked about, then snapped the padlock
Open and shut again.
She slumped against my chest.
I came to meet Him half way.
He didn't come, Isabel. Your father is waiting for me.
Have you seen Him?

Who, God?

Yes.

The tool-shed door blew shut.
We stumbled over fallen tree limbs.
Get inside, Mother. We'll see Him soon enough.
Suddenly Mother seemed frail and thin.
I urged her to eat plain bread with lukewarm milk.

By noon the wind subsided.
Neighbors emerged from their homes
To inspect the damage.
I brushed Mother's matted wet hair,
And helped her into a dry gown,
You'll be fine, Mother.
Just stay here while I try to clean up the mess.

That night I was so tired I cried.
For days we would not have electricity.
I bathed in the shallow bit of water in our tub,
The same water used later for laundry.

Where was David?
Coward! Coward! Coward!
And Gilbert.
Dear delicate Gilbert with his pure sweet voice.

So what that he brought pleasure to the masses.
This was no time for pleasure, for beautiful music.
I needed help. I needed my father!

In the aftermath of the storm Mother improved.
From time to time cheerful, almost lucid.
Other times dark and brooding,
Calling on God.
Please God, come get me, she said.
I've been expecting you.

She was my responsibility now.
She the child, I the mother.
I was afraid to kiss her goodnight, or get too near
Afraid she would never recover
But cast a spell, then disappear.

Liberation

Liberation

Mother and I lived a nightmare of darkness,
Her visions angry and sad.
I, too, dreamed ghastly dreams
But nothing like those she had.
She moaned, her voice climbing the scale
Until I raced to her bed, and shook her.
Wake up, Mother, it's one of your nightmares again.
Even a nightmare comes to an end.

While living underground, gradually blind,
We felt our way back from the slimy mine,
Our blood icy and thin.
We did not smile, there was no reason to smile
In mile after mile of darkness.
We did not appreciate the beauty of light until then.
We'd been in a cave but emerged again
To the rest of the world,

A brilliant world alive with laughter and love.
Our breakthrough arrived with the mail.
David wondered if he was wanted back.
Wanted?
We scrubbed the welcome mat
And Mother wrote David that
We were too excited to sleep,
A nonfiction fairy tale.
David would be home soon.
Seated at the table in his usual chair.
David would hang the doors,
Put new siding on the shed
And anything else that needed repair.
David would do everything he could
To put the house in order.

And, as if David's homecoming weren't enough,
Gilbert phoned from Paris, a break in his busy routine.
Mother was ecstatic,
Her baby would take time between performances
To return home.
All of Miami would rejoice.
One of its own famous, his voice a passport to stardom.

Mother woke from her stupor
To help me prepare for my brothers.
Their bedrooms aired and cleaned,
Cupboards filled with delicacies.
Mother danced from chair to chair, room to room,
They're coming, Isabel.
You've worked so hard.
We'll celebrate with a party in our own back yard.

You mean for David and his friends, I asked.

No, for music lovers and other guests.
At the auditorium, then, the reception hall,
Or the lobby. You're right.
Our yard wouldn't hold them all.

For the past few years Gilbert's name was broadcast
On the evening news.
Talented, Gifted, Internationally acclaimed,
Local opera star in demand
My baby brother,
Now accustomed to fame,
Was coming home.

But David, the other half of childhood,
Was coming as well.
I answered his letter:
   How can I tell if it's you?
   Wear a carnation in your lapel.
   We can hardly wait. Have you changed?
   Mother and I rearranged your bedroom.
   We had your guitar restrung last year.
   Hurry! We are overcome with happiness.
We had just sunk lower than low,
And now David and Gilbert were here.

Awkward and shy, David wore a beard
His clothes a different cut than other men wore
Khaki and leather,
His skin a darker tan than it was before.
Laughter came easy.

But early in the day
He fell silent, with nothing more to say.
He laced his boots, smoothed his pants
Picked at non-existent lint.

Gilbert gave notice he and his agent would stay
In a room downtown, at a big hotel
We'd dine as his guests at a posh café.
His hair was long, his cheeks almost white
Fingernails manicured, blue eyes bright.
A stranger, uneasy in the family circle.

Mother couldn't help but stroke their faces
Her hands constantly reaching for them
Wanting a hug.
David shrugged. *New draperies?*

Yes, Mother said.

Your hair looks different. Did you have it cut?

Yes. I believe so, yes.

Isabel, are you sure you haven't lost weight?
Isn't our mother looking great?

I turned to Gilbert, who dominated the room.
My friends are excited.
They remember when you tagged along
When you were afraid of the moon.

Nothing's changed, he said.
But none of that's true.
I was never afraid of the moon, were you?
We've all changed, for better or worse.
Gilbert didn't stay long, he had to rehearse
For the concert tomorrow.

Later that night David checked Dad's old fishing tackle

And oiled two or three reels.

Suppose there's still a silk tie I can borrow?

I don't want to embarrass little brother tomorrow,

We spent most of the day on the telephone.

Newspaper reporters, booking agents

Friends from London and Rome, most of them women.

I wore black, cut dangerously low

And shared David with Mother,

Dressed in a new long-sleeved lace

With pearls Dad gave her years ago.

I held up a program for all to see.

And pointed to the stage.

Our brother, I said.

Soon the auditorium lights were dimmed,
There, in a blinding spotlight, was Gilbert.
Mother wanted to wave to him,
But David took her hand. *Later, Mom.*

Every seat was filled, the auditorium crowded
Gilbert's opening number a simple song,
Sweet, clear and unwavering.
Applause was loud.
After a couple of arias guaranteed
To bring down the house,
Gilbert was no longer ours.

At intermission Mother checked with the caterer.
More guests than we thought. I hope you came prepared.
Everyone who was anyone,
Everyone in music was there.

The chef assured Mother.
No need to worry,
Plenty of lobster and champagne.
If we run low, we'll hurry out to get more.

At the end of Gilbert's final number,
I clapped louder than anyone else,
That's our brother, I shouted again.
We couldn't believe Gilbert's talent and charm.
This is David, my other brother,
And this is our mother on David's arm.

Half the attendees remained for the reception,
Most of them headed for the bar.
Others lined up to shake Gilbert's hand.
We remember you as a child, you've come so far.

David and I were reaching for a tray of drinks
When, descending the stairs nearby,
Were a stooped old man and his frayed wife
Vaguely familiar, but I didn't know why
A fat old lady, a gray-haired man.
The woman twirling a Japanese fan,
Our piano teacher, of course, Mrs. Florence Getz,
The gentleman, her husband,
With the aid of a walking cane.

David stiffened and turned his back.
But just at that moment Mother appeared
And led us to Gilbert.
Dear, this is Miami's best piano instructor.
In her glory, Mrs. Getz sighed,
Then touched Gilbert's throat and hair.
She flapped her fan.
Angelic, your voice. I heard you did Rodolpho
In Madrid or Milan. Such genius is rare.

Mr. Getz made his way to a velvet sofa.

And fell with a heavy plunk.

He coughed and wheezed.

Alcohol is poison to an old man like me.

It's been years, when I could handle maybe two or three.

David suggested he needed one now.

He laughed and leaned forward,

Not even one, young man, I wouldn't know how.

If not even one, two or three it'll be.

A man of your discretion deserves the best.

Mr. Getz protested, but soon guzzled Scotch.

Next David delivered a tray of cakes.

Two or three, Mr. Getz, whatever it takes

To actually taste the delicious frosting.

Pastries baked by a famous chef.

Never one to deny himself

The company of celebrated guests,

Mr. Getz drank and ate, five or six.

His face turned red, hands shaky.

He wiped a stained handkerchief across his lips,

But ate another pastry, drank another Scotch.

Soon Mother and Mrs. Getz approached.

Oh there you are. We wondered where you had gone.

Mrs. Getz waved her fan.

Such a splendid melody, that second song.

Tired of Mrs. Getz, Mother agreed,

She needed to return to the guest of honor, her son.

Mrs. Getz told Mr. Getz to get out his keys.

They needed to leave, or rue the day.

People their age weren't used to the late hour,

Mr. Getz argued he would rather stay a few minutes more.

As they left, David winked.

The party had thinned to a few old friends.

Mother danced and swirled in her lacy dress.

Her cheeks flushed with excitement,

Her party a big success.

Gilbert kissed her, and then said goodbye.

He was due in New York for Madame Butterfly.

The following afternoon,
Mother struggled for air.
She was reading the late edition's glowing reports
Of Gilbert's recital, and the catered affair,
A dozen flattering adjectives,
When a much shorter item caught her eye.
Mr. and Mrs. Getz killed in a highway accident,
On their way from the county auditorium.
Apparently Mr. Getz, at the wheel,
Suffered from a diabetic seizure.
Mother lowered the paper. *Can this be true?*

Reading the news over Mother's shoulder, David stirred.
He placed a forefinger to his lips and whispered.
That's two.

Oxygen, I needed oxygen!
Brroom-brroom
I'd been holding my breath since the night before,
The rumble of drumbeats faded now.
A lifetime of fear reduced to ashes, like a meteor.

I wanted to escape then, with Gilbert
Who answered the call of music,
Adored, regaled,
Hearing nothing but applause
Giving nothing but pleasure.
Or with David, his own man,
Willing to chuck it all,
Who would never be rich, adored, regaled
His wealth measured on a different scale.

From time to time, for an hour or a day
My brothers passed through town
On their way to some other place.
Neither of their futures tied down,
They would pause long enough to visit Mother,
Sign a birthday card,
Treat us to dinner,
But never take root, never settle in,
Never an emotional link in the family again.
I wrote them both.
And added a special note for David.
Thank you.

Oh, to retrieve the weightless feathers shed
And left behind, blown hither and yon.
Who were we then?
Who are we now?
We simply dress our wounds somehow,
Consult the stars, and drift on.

About the Author

Mary May Burruss spent her childhood and most of her adult life in southern, sultry Miami. As a child playing with paper-dolls, her imagination wandered where it pleased. Her fragile, one-dimensional friends lived in royal palaces and took part in wild adventures. Today, Mary May lives in Cape Canaveral, a place where rockets roar and imagination touches the stars. Her half-fantasy world has no rules, no limits on creative storytelling. Many of Mary May's poems and short stories have been published and recognized. In workshops in Miami and, now in Cocoa Beach, Mary May has inspired and mentored a community of novices and accomplished writers striving to improve in their craft.

Sunspots is based on the truth then embellished to protect her loved ones.

Made in the USA